COUNTRY
MADNESS

COUNTRY
MADNESS

AN ENGLISH COUNTRY DIARY
OF A SINGAPOREAN PSYCHIATRIST

Ong Yong Lock

monsoon

monsoonbooks

Published in 2010
by Monsoon Books Pte Ltd
52 Telok Blangah Road, #03-05 Telok Blangah House
Singapore 098829
www.monsoonbooks.com.sg

ISBN: 978-981-08-5432-4

Cover painting©Wang Jianan and Cai Xiaoli
All paintings (except *Eight Fairies* p.69)©Wang Jianan and Cai Xiaoli;
Eight Fairies©Wang Jia Jia

National Library Board, Singapore Cataloguing-in-Publication Data
Ong, Yong Lock.
Country madness : an English country diary of a Singaporean
psychiatrist / Ong Yong Lock. – Singapore : Monsoon Books, 2010.
p. cm.
Includes bibliographical references.
ISBN-13 : 978-981-08-5432-4 (pbk.)

1. Ong, Yong Lock. 2. Psychiatrists – England – Norfolk – Biography.
3. Singaporeans – England – Norfolk – Biography.
4. Norfolk (England) – Social life and customs. 5. Norfolk (England) –
Biography – Humor. I. Title.

RC438.6
616.890092 -- dc22   OCN607969519

Printed in Singapore
15 14 13 12 11 10   1 2 3 4 5

This book is dedicated to my parents
and
J.K. Eltringham
I wish you were all standing beside me

and
for my mentor in Chinese Art,
Puan Sri Esther Tan

and
my muse
Carolyn

Contents

Acknowledgements

I owe a debt of gratitude to lawyer, author and artist Wong Swee Hoon, a.k.a. youngest sister's husband's elder sister. Without her I would not have made contact with my editor Richard Alan Lord.

Richard continues to be my weather vane, directing me in all the right directions and from my typhoon of thought-disordered ideas, he creates a gentle breeze of coherent thoughts and words.

Finally the greatest debt and thanks to my publisher Monsoon Books, without whom there would be no book.

And a big thanks too to all my readers. Using Richard's words 'We offer our readers this book in the full spirit of friendship and collegiality.'

Illustrations

All paintings by Wang Jianan and Cai Xiaoli except *Eight Fairies*, painted by Wang Jia Jia.

Preamble

'Obsessional neurosis is the consequence of a pre-sexual sexual pleasure which is later transformed into (self)-reproach.'
Letter of Freud to Fleiss, 15 October 1895

'To be interested in the changing seasons is a happier state of mind then to be hopelessly in love with spring.'
George Santayana (1863–1952)

This book takes up a number of themes I wish to explore at a decorously slight depth. This journey will allow me to:

• examine the impact of living in an adopted country, in its rural countryside;
• reconsider relevant symbols and motifs from my native country;
• retell tales from my childhood that I have never grown tired of, now told through the voice of a psychiatrist;
• and weave all these strands together into a cohesive framework of many thoughts and themes.

Above all, this is a record of a growing love for the differences and similarities of two cultures. This growth has reached a statistically significant level and hence demanded of me the writing of a book. I decided on the framework of dividing this book into chapters based on the seasons so that I would not be accused of being obsessional and writing under the one generic heading of English weather. I will try to uncover my themes in concordance with the rhythm of changing seasons rather than a season. Perhaps a decision I may regret and may have to move into a mode of self-reproach. (What would Freud say to this?) Up to now, I have only written thematic scientific papers with scrupulously causal links between facts. Now I find myself trying to write about talismanic correlations, which may turn out to be a problematic exercise.

The pomposity of the above paragraphs reflects my acquired self. My traditional self squirms in embarrassment when reading it as I am not really a weaver of words, but a metallurgist shaping and smashing shards of words to make them fit coherently. However, I have managed to write a half-dozen chapters and think I now have a book. The essence of each chapter is captured in one, or at the most two, paintings, thus contributing to the debate between scholars on the power of words versus visual art. Do paintings or words have the ascendancy in stimulating the minds of literati? The everlasting argument continues as always and ever shall be unto the age of ages. Amen.

My painting skills are not of a standard to be used as illustrations. (Many will say that my writing skills are below the required standard too, but I do have an ability to dream.) The task of creating the required paintings was therefore delegated to a Chinese husband and wife team. Both are painters, back then recently migrated from China as they wanted to flex their artistic muscles and explore the challenging art world of London. They agreed to take on the project.

One illustration here is by their son, a child at the time of commissioning the paintings, now a graduate of a major London art school. Tradition still lives in most Chinese families. The artists and I spent many happy hours discussing the variables each painting should capture. They have achieved these targets through combining their learning of English culture and their traditional values. The freshness of their new understanding encouraged father, mother and son to sink roots in westernised Elysian Fields.

Let me give you a little personal background. I grew up in Singapore, a busy Southeast Asian city. Postgraduate training required a transfer to London, an even busier city. Singapore prides herself on a comforting sense of order and contains risks; London is chaotic and embraces risks. A career change a few years later dictated another move, this time to Norfolk. I arrived totally unprepared for full-time country living, my free-floating anxiety completely at its peak and out of control. This was based on the lack of support from friends who dismissed my relocation plan. I had survived weekending, or rather spending weekends in Wiltshire, which proved refreshing and rejuvenating. But my friends' prediction about my living full-time in the country was that it was a poorly thought-out career plan as they perceived me to be an urbane man who could only exist in cities, even though I was equipped with psychological defences and insight.

In rural Norfolk, the umbilical cord to city living was definitely and forcefully severed. I found myself desperately lonely and physically, frightfully cold. Every defence mechanism, and I had many of them, was slowly breaking down. A cacophony of conflicts reverberated through my soul. To prevent a total breakdown and a plunge into a psychotic state, I looked for redemption. It came in the shape of a quintessential English woman and the Fifth Season.

Carolyn and I met in a pub in Wareham. It was the second week of September, when summer was starting to fade and autumn had not yet established its hold. Some Chinese scholars recognise this fleeting, abbreviated time as the Fifth Season. I did not know what to expect. She was my London solicitor's cousin and a much-needed new social contact. We ate, parried and questioned.

I admitted to a lack of interest in hunting, fishing, shooting, gardening and amateur dramatics. These were apparently the country pursuits favoured by Carolyn and some of her greatest passions. A desperate animation entered into her body language in order to cover her despair. In response, I felt a stirring within me which I diagnosed, medically as well, as my under-used libido. We correctly promised to meet again, and as I waited to respond to 'you must come over for drinks or dinner sometime ...' (the traditional English social closure which is often not followed through), I experienced the continuing sense of cultural disruption.

That evening, sitting and staring at the Chinese carpet from my parents' home, clutching a *stengah* of scotch and listening to the reassuring rhythm of ice clinking against fine facets of cut glass, I began to examine the excitable feelings experienced since lunch. It was certainly not just sexual feeling heading towards sudden tumescence. It had to be, and has proved to be, the gestational coalescing and coming together of the Chinese in me and my adopted wondrous English countryside. My own many-splendoured thing.

Dr Han Suyin, a medical doctor, wrote her book entitled *A Many-Splendoured Thing*. This book became a major Hollywood movie and spawned a theme song sung by almost every other contestant in local Talent-time contests in Singapore and Malaysia in the Sixties. These contests were the forerunner of today's shows seeking to identify Pop Idols. The song still gets an occasional airing on the radio and at karaoke clubs.

Dr Han herself at once became the muse and mentor of generations of writers trying to explore trans-cultural issues and to give sense to intercultural conflicts and experiences. In a similar vein, her mentees continue to explore the dichotomy of backgrounds. Mixed race, conflict, feelings of inferiority, superiority, shame, regret.

Dr Han's book mainly, though, describes her reawakening of passion after a bereavement. Her great sadness is replaced by an awareness of being able to feel desire again. In lyrical prose, Dr Han describes the moment when, as a dedicated widow, she meets her many-splendoured thing. She writes that she *feels* rather than sees the emblems of happy augury woven on the carpet supporting her new love's face as he lay on the floor. Something within her moved and stirred. She goes on to write a seminal book.

I owe our family doctor the causal link I have to Dr Han as he shared the medical on-call rota at Hong Kong's main hospital with her during her reawakening. He disclosed to me how he and other junior doctors had to cover her duties when she went off to meet her new love. I am sure none of them complained, as they felt they were all colleagues and contributors to a momentous event.

I wish I could express myself as Dr Han does, as I experienced a similar sensation when the traditional Chinese symbols representing good luck (peonies, double-edged swords, princes and sacred fungi) woven on my parents' carpet leapt out at me and jostled into my consciousness. Write a book!

AUSPICIOUS CARPET SYMBOLS
(SEE PLATE I)

Elizabeth Lawrence, a garden designer and author who left a legacy of her garden for research and to be admired, insists that everyone must take time to sit and watch the leaves turn. I did, often, taking a leaf out of her book, and watched leaves turn. This may have also stimulated writing this book with chapters held together by the seasons, as I too have been seduced by the English obsession with weather.

I will admit that I now treasure the changes of seasons wherever I choose to live. Each season brings its own peculiarities: magical, stimulating, ever-changing, refreshing. I am aware of a distinct change in my own mood linked with the seasons. This I had not experienced while living in the tropics. But having lived in Britain, I now have a particular empathy with patients who have cyclical mood swings correlated to seasons.

In the United Kingdom, everyone talks incessantly about weather and this proclivity travels with the English when they migrate abroad. I remember my parents' expatriate friends in Singapore saying things like: 'The monsoon is extremely early this season?'; 'Perhaps we are between the awful monsoons?'; 'This climate is far, far too hot, we need the winter (!) monsoon to cool us down?'; 'When will the monsoon come to end this long hot summer?(!)'. Amongst Singaporeans themselves, the monsoons are hardly mentioned. It is a charming English compulsion to couch an almost fixed climate with romantic metrological terminology.

On an island republic two degrees north of the equator, weather is constant and predictable. It comes in two flavours: hot, humid and dry, or hot, humid and wet. Perhaps this is why Singaporeans do not talk much about the weather. They have a major passion for food with a spectrum of flavours and so to discuss a subject limited to just two flavours? *Aiyoh!*

But a fascination with the seasons spurred my own awakening, a stirring and moving towards a nervous acceptance of the imagery of my rural surroundings becoming my own many-splendoured thing of 'many things Chinese in the English countryside.' My story is a narrative leading readers to capture and perhaps empathise with these unique feelings.

It all starts in the Fifth Season.

·

The Fifth Season

'The seasons are what a symphony ought to be: four perfect
movements in harmony with each other.'
Arthur Rubenstein (1887–1982)

'Basic to Chinese culture and mythology is the principle of
the 5 "hsing", "elements" or "stages of harmonious change".'
A *feng shui* principle (circa West Han Dynasty)

I met Carolyn in the Fifth Season of my first year in Norfolk.
This propitious meeting led to a major train of thoughts used for
the foundation of this book and created its form and structure.
Having a strong obsessional trait to my personality, I have
to write, record and describe every detail. Now is the time for
Carolyn and seasons.

Some Chinese scholars believe in a fifth season as five is an
important number in Chinese numerology. It is uneven, disruptive,
traditionally considered male (of course). The number four and
the universally accepted four seasons is gentle, perfect, rational,
complete as exhibited in the geometrical proportions of squares
and rectangles. Yet most Chinese dislike the sound of the word
four, as phonetically it could be mistaken for the Mandarin word

for 'death'. (This holds true for several other dialects as well.)

Amongst Chinese, there is a superstitious avoidance of buying a house numbered four or forty-four: 'death tenfold'. Indeed, where I live in Singapore, at number thirty-six, there is a neighbour at thirty-eight and then a leap to numbering the next house number forty-two. Furthermore, it is not uncommon at Chinese wedding banquets to leave out numbering banqueting tables with the numbers four, forty and, especially, forty-four so as to avoid inviting 'less good' karma to the nuptial ceremony.

In the early days of Chairman Mao's regime, the Great Helmsman reacted to the feudal Four Old Things: old culture, old customs, old habits and old ways of thinking. Revolutionary thinking powered the Communist surge and was initially welcomed by the populace. A tsunami of destruction of antiques, paintings, customs and religion wreaked heavy casualties. There would have been even greater loss if the Communist movement had moved on to add a fifth variable. However, they stayed and played with four and death.

A few officials in today's China demand the return of the 'Admonitions of the Instructress to Court Ladies' scroll from the British Museum. This is similar in request to the Greek government demanding the return to Greece of the Elgin Marbles. The Admonition scroll by Ku'K'ai-chih is thought to be the oldest painted Chinese scroll, predating the Tang dynasty and an invaluable benchmark for early Chinese paintings. There have been other artefacts put up for sale by collectors in major auction houses that are deemed China's lawful heritage pilfered by Western pirates. Hang on, stop, sit, reflect. How many treasures from aeons of Chinese dynasties were lost during the destruction of the Four Old Things?

Most people are aware of the notorious Gang of Four. This was the treacherous political faction led by Madame Mao, the Helmsman's infamous wife, which wreaked further chaos during the Cultural Revolution. The jury is still out as to whether decisions were made by Mao and actions then channelled through the Gang of Four, or whether the Gang was entirely autonomous. All four were ultimately charged with treason. Once again, here we see the number four as unlucky creating a breeding ground of turmoil. Less is known of the Little Gang of Four, a conservative group who stood against Deng Xiaoping. All four of these dissidents fell from grace too and were demoted within party ranks.

Enough of the troublesome four. Let's just affirm that five is a good number, a number of symbolic tranquillity that links a harmony of change between the two seasons of summer and autumn.

There is often a fifth season in England, commonly known as Indian summer. It is a time when the Earth clings doggedly onto unseasonal warmth and maintains its delicious dappled light before giving in to autumn. It is often, too, the time when there is an outpouring of comments about conflicting emotions. (Unusual for the English, who are renowned for keeping their confidences to themselves.) They talk about a sadness at the shortening of days and the loss of light struggling against the safety of being cocooned in long, dark nights and drawn curtains.

My psychiatric colleagues interpret this unusual behaviour as prodromal symptoms to the autumnal peak of depressive illness and to a syndrome fittingly named SAD (Seasonal Affective Disorder). Taking my cue from the usual behaviour of the English, I do not trade one confidence for another although I know the correct diagnosis: the disruptive 'Fifth Season syndrome'.

During my childhood, I diligently learnt and recited (or perhaps I should say, regurgitated without any understanding of the concepts involved) the curious rhythms of the seasons as described by Robert Louis Stevenson:

> *In winter, I get up at night*
> *And dress by yellow candle light.*
> *In summer, quite the other way,*
> *I have to go to bed by day.*
> *I have to go to bed and see*
> *The birds still hopping on the tree*
> *Or hear the grown-up people's feet*
> *Still going past me in the street.*

I did not understand then the import of the seasons. Seasons were a curriculum topic we learnt about at school, something that occurred in temperate climates. The only seasons we knew (and eagerly anticipated) were the seasons of the different fruits: durians, rambutans, cikus, mangosteens, lychees. Imagine my amazement when I discovered the enchantment of living in the cycle with four established seasons and then to discover that there was a fifth. All fleeting, momentary and truly magical.

Was it retaliation against, or reparation for, my early ignorance of images I was unable to comprehend that punitively made me teach my Scottish goddaughter Anna the childish jingle of five elements; images she would find likewise difficult to comprehend?

> *Water produces Wood but destroys Fire;*
> *Fire produces Earth but destroys Metal;*
> *Metal produces Water but destroys Wood;*
> *Wood produces Fire but destroys Earth;*
> *Earth produces Metal but destroys Water.*

Anna, when she grew up, would tease me not over the imagery, but for teaching her a jingle which she insisted did not rhyme in English. In retribution, to dilute my paranoia of colonial oppression, she would sing a song, sung to her great great-grandfather by an English lord sometime in the 1930s which contained rhyming Chinesey couplets:

From Wu Chow Wu, I come makee walkee
One piece ship, two piecey bamboo
Inside he no belong, outside he lop-long
all welly nice and ploper can do
Hi yi ya, chin chin chin
Chow chow welly good my likee he
Makee plenty sing song, savy by and by
Chinaman he welly good, he laugh hi-ya
Chinese cookie, she welly nicey
She live in kitchen topsidey house
Takee little pussy cat and ee little bow-wow
Welly nice pot stew boil with a mouse
Hi yi ya ...

By this stage, Anna is always unable to complete her song as she falls over with laughter. I am not amused and give thanks for the current vogue of political correctness. No more chinoiserie coolie songs. Anna and I decide to cement our cultural bonding by commissioning a painting of an elegant Chinese man and woman courting in adjoining houses: not topsy-turvy, nor topsidey, as this would ultimately redress the nonsensical words we have learnt from each other. Once again, a painting will exert its superior position over words!

Unfortunately, the suggestion results in a painting more kitsch than courtly: a scene of two balconies with star-crossed lovers. Anna and I fall over each other with laughter. The artists are not amused. They were assigned a task with clear instructions and the painting was as commissioned. But something had been lost in translation, which often happens in intercultural relationships. Resulting, in this instance, in all being let down by words, hues, visual images and a serious failure of humour! Ah yes, another convergence of four elements.

THE BALCONY SCENE
(SEE PLATE II)

Autumn

*'It was one of those perfect autumnal days which occur
more frequently in memory than in life.'*
P.D. James (1920–)

And this is my personal account of autumn, the first full chapter of my delusional tapestry. When every leaf is a flower. (I owe this simple, enchanting notion to the philosopher and author Albert Camus. He couples this idea with autumn being another spring, a companion thought which is perhaps just as existential.)

As mentioned earlier, my Southeast Asian homeland hosts two barely distinguishable seasons. However, if global warming changes the unvarying weather, Singaporeans may then start to discuss weather, though probably in sci-fi terminology as monstrous lizards and other creatures start to walk across the island. Another Galapagos?

Which leads me to the consideration of another English obsession: their love and passionate care for their pets in particular, and animals in general, sometimes to the disadvantage of their fellow humans. I have sat holding the hands of several friends at the death of a pet cat or dog. Strong alpha-males who would keep a stiff upper lip under any other circumstance dissolve quietly into tears. My female friends expect me to administer bereavement therapy throughout episodes of noisy sobbing when their pets pass away.

The Norfolk countryside shelters a menagerie of magical animals: pheasants, foxes, partridges, jade moon rabbits and three-legged toads. There are also the usual livestock: sheep, cows, pigs, horses and all description of fowl. Now according to Chinese folklore, the timeless trinity of a full moon, rabbit and toad marks autumn; a trinity easily identified in the English countryside. I meet my mythical jade rabbits (also known as moon rabbits) on most misty autumnal mornings. I look for them on nights around mid-autumn when the moon is at its greatest distance from earth and apparently perfectly round. Indeed, I see the full trinity of the moon as all Chinese have since 2000 BCE. This does not require any leap of faith on my part, as the moon and its companions are deeply embedded in the Chinese psyche.

The basis for this belief is the story of a beautiful maiden called Chang'é which many of us grew up with. Before she gained her fame as the reigning Moon Goddess of the Mid-Autumn Festival, she laboured as a mere mortal. According to the legend, she married an archer who had the reputation of being an unusually powerful and deadly accurate shot. His arrows flew faster, further and, invariably, straight to the bullseye. Due to this amazing skill, he was frequently away from home, summoned by the gods to deal with catastrophes requiring the skill of an archer. There are several stories written about his feats and adventures.

Chang'é resented being left on her own so often. A conflict of emotions disrupted her mood. She felt rejected, yet very much loved, bullied and also treasured by her husband. Being low in spirits, she had to strike back. On one of his visits home, Chang'é noticed a pill in her husband's quiver of arrows. Could this be the source of his ability? In retaliation for his seemingly erratic behaviour, she swallowed the pill. Suddenly and surely, she was flying. Soaring above the clouds, she ultimately landed on the moon. Dishevelled and gasping from exhaustion, she coughed up the pill which turned instantly into a jade rabbit. She herself then changed into a three-legged toad. The moon therefore harbours within its autumnal circumference both toad and rabbit and shines on as the legendary trinity.

I have been trained over the years of writing scientific papers to include only relevant, reliable and evidence-based facts in my papers. So imagine my delight in being able to recount the above tale free of all scientific restraint. I am allowed to write a paragraph that begs belief. The casual link and possible correlation between a pill, arrows, flight and transfiguration are highly suspect, to say the least. In any event, definitely not evidence-based. The sadistic streak in the mind of the original teller of this legendary mythical lore may need further psychological exploration. A bored housewife flies to the moon, turns into a toad and is incarcerated for the rest of her life with a rabbit in a limited changing space. New, quarter, half and full. A judgment perhaps too severe to be served on the idle curiosity and restless behaviour of a neglected wife?

Unfortunately, rabbits, jade moon or real, are becoming an endangered species. There is an illness called myxomatosis, occasionally rampant in the countryside, that targets rabbits and reduces the rabbit population significantly.

In Norfolk, rabbits are further at risk from the huntress Carolyn. She wields an air rifle, often poised to take shots at rabbits chewing leafy herbs in her herb garden. (Rabbits have fine palates, as they enjoy pungent coriander, sage and basil.) Thankfully, Carolyn is a poor shot.

It is difficult to work out this behavioural pattern of hers as Carolyn also has a great love of animals. Her dogs Pickles and

Chutney have been my nemeses because of the indulgence she lavishes on them, and yet she is prepared to go out and shoot defenceless little bunnies! For what, their occasional munching on her garden's largesse? Herbs can easily be bought in supermarkets.

But culturally mixed relationships do tend to have more difficulties than those with partners from the same culture. Intercultural partners have different benchmarks and values to navigate. Subtleties of language and humour are frequently lost in translation. A strong trans-cultural relationship requires infinite patience and a continuing show of good manners to each other. Thus, I encourage Carolyn with her shooting, reassured by her poor marksmanship and confidence that, in any event, my jade moon rabbits will not be harmed by her.

This narrative now moves on to more animal stories and folkloric tales, all tied somehow to autumn.

We were on an exhilarating walk when we met our neighbour, a farmer. He informed us that he had just shot the vixen that had been wreaking carnage amongst his free-range hens. I was about to share with him that on several mornings, whilst driving to work, the sight of bloodied feathers and mutilated carcasses in the hen pens disrupted the good *feng shui* for my working day. On such days, nothing had worked smoothly. Patients, nurses and other members of the multidisciplinary team were more challenging than usual. The working equilibrium of the day would, at best, be unpredictable.

He stuck his hand out. I responded with mine, thinking I was going to offer him a congratulatory handshake. To my anguish, I instead found myself holding the tail of the vixen with the rest of the animal hanging downwards before me: cold, dead, in a state of rigor mortis.

Wahayee! Wahayee! A shriek started to reverberate in the depths of my larynx. My uvula began beating an involuntary tempo which would surely result in a piercing, shuddering scream. But Chinese men, being inscrutable, do not lose their composure. My mind started scanning defence mechanisms to control the growing hysteria and landed securely on a fable of the Fox Woman. Almost immediately, the vixen in my hand felt somewhat benign as she was transformed into a fairy tale character. In Chinese legend, foxes are known to have an erotic quality because:

- at age fifty, they become women;
- at a hundred years, they revert into young girls;
- when they reach a thousand years, they attain the status of 'Celestial Fox' and gain admission to the Halls of the Sun and the Moon.

In this legend, there is a young scholar who is distracted each night from his books by a stunningly adorable girl. Before long, he makes love to her constantly. She is insatiable. He becomes weaker and increasingly debilitated, far more than is explicable in physiological terms. A monk informs him the girl is actually a fox who is sucking his youth to achieve celestial status. The scholar kills his beauty and she immediately transforms into a vixen ... cold, dead and in a state of rigor mortis before him. Freud often proclaimed that the two driving forces of life are sex and aggression. In this story, the narrative is driven by both variables, neatly bonded together.

I hand back the now celestial-like fox to our neighbour, mumble a congratulatory sound and pull Carolyn sharply away. She looks shell-shocked too, and for once is not the pompous harridan she can be about my need to empathise with the rituals of the English countryside. In response to this episode, I again commissioned yet another painting. This one to depict Carolyn and my equally balanced partnership. The artists know us well as a couple and, interestingly, capture this in the body language of one of the figures, showing a higher controlling hand ...

THE HARRIDAN
(SEE PLATE III)

Like the peacock, the male pheasant is a very attractively feathered bird. The female pheasant and peahen share a similar feathery dowdiness. As pheasants race across the flat fields of Norfolk, their feathers a rich palette of ambers, browns, greys and reds set against green grass, they look like mythological phoenixes. I have been reliably informed by a set of Norfolk ornithologists (a.k.a. 'twitchers') that the Chinese golden pheasant, a prototype of the phoenix, was introduced to the English countryside where it bred with other indigenous species to produce the magnificent present-day bird. Legend has it that phoenixes supposedly only appeared at times of empowering peace. However, for me personally, pheasants have been a source of crippling disruption. This next incident will serve as one prime example.

In the fading light of an autumnal evening, I arrived home, ragged and burnt-out by a day of complex patients, complaining relatives, and suffering from the early Seasonal Affective Disorder, or late Fifth Season syndrome, to ... a still-life composition of a brace of dead pheasants on my kitchen table worthy of Flemish master Frans Snijders. Lying dead and cold before me. *Aiyoh! Aiyoh!*

Stuck between their claws was a white envelope. Death moncy? Death seemed to be stalking me as one of my patients earlier in the day had attempted to take his own life.

Despite my flagging energy levels, I began screaming in terror. This behaviour pattern of shrieking and screaming was fast becoming part of my country persona. The telephone rang; a familiar voice. When she established my bout of hyperventilation was not due to an asthmatic attack, but a panic attack of symbolic death supposedly stalking me, Carolyn coldly told me to cover the birds with a tea cloth, blot out the image and control my stupidity.

I did so, though I would have preferred that she talk me through the process instead of ringing off immediately. Gingerly, I extracted the white envelope to discover a note. My cleaning lady's husband, a beater in the local shoot, had generously given me this brace of pheasants to dine on and enjoy with friends. This was not, as I had assumed, an omen from the grim reaper. A foolish misinterpretation on my part.

For the next few days, I circumnavigated the pantry as the birds solemnly swung from a hook. They had to be hung for days to produce better cooking flavour. Thankfully, none of my patients made suicide attempts by hanging (or otherwise) during this time. In childish remonstration, I turned the painting of Carolyn and myself, commissioned in a moment of presumed equality, to face the wall.

At last, the birds were ready and my cleaning lady and her sister-in-law plucked the pheasants for a scrumptious dinner party. They challenged me to say very, very, very quickly 'pleasant peasant pheasant plucker'. Everyone should try this. I repeat it to Carolyn, who in pique, drawing herself into full country lady stature, says all jingles are childish. What? I recite the non-childlike jingle of five elements in retaliation.

A second pheasant story: domiciliary assessments for older patients living in a rural setting are a practical method of providing good necessary care for this patient group. On a misty autumnal morning, driving between the homes of different patients, I stopped my car to allow safe passage for the pheasant as it crossed the narrow country lane. Its markings were particularly beautiful and my appreciation for its similarities to a phoenix was reinforced. It stopped mid-lane, stared, ruffled its splendid feathers of browns and gold, then moved on. I slowly accelerated forward and heard a sickening thud. The pheasant had decided to backtrack.

I have now learnt that pheasants have an (apparently deserved) reputation for being stupid birds. What! What! What! This bird was descended from the noble phoenix? Phoenixes could never have been perceived as stupid. They were embroidered on ceremonial robes and banners. A stupid bird would never have been thus honoured. Something in the interbreeding in the English countryside must have caused this permutation, resulting in an intellectually challenged gene.

PHOENIX PAPER CUT
(SEE PLATE IV)

According to long-honoured countryside rules:

- The driver who hits a pheasant drives on.
- The next driver to arrive at the scene of the roadkill claims the spoils for the dinner table.

I drove on, spurred by my guilt of having damaged such a beautiful bird. But then the Hippocratic oath taken at the time of my graduation stopped me. I turned back. The pheasant was shuddering in spasms, coloured feathers splintered into shards of broken browns and golds, gradually tinged with a slow seeping stream of blood red. Remembering the oath 'to cure sometimes, to treat occasionally and to comfort always', I calmly and collectedly started to put the bird out of its misery by breaking its neck. This was in contrast to—indeed, out of synch with—my usual hysteria when dealing with all things country. Despite my firmly wringing the bird's neck and hearing the sound of crunching vertebrae between my fists, the bird refused to die.

Two cars drove by, their drivers throwing suspicious looks in my direction as if to suggest I was breaking the roadkill code and being a foreign poacher camouflaged in a pinstriped grey suit and tie. 'To comfort always'; and in response, I made the decision to drive the bird to a butcher in the nearest village who would competently put it out of its suffering. I gently laid the bird next to me and started to drive. But then a sudden shrug and a flickering lowering of its red-hooded eyes put the bird and me out of our collective pain. For the next couple of weeks however, Carolyn deliberately tried to drive into a female pheasant so we could have a brace for another dinner party!

This book has been identified by friends as belonging to the genre of coffee-table tomes. In other words, decorative and insubstantial. (They expected in-depth psychological correlations. Yikes!) Apparently, all coffee-table books must contain recipes. A current vogue. I am not sure how to cook pheasant, other than that it involves cider, thyme and apples.

For a new challenge, I will now attempt to give the recipe for baking moon cakes, a delectable treat baked to mark the Mid-Autumn Festival. Round in shape to emulate the moon, they are decorated with pastry images of, yes, rabbits and toads, and filled with a floating myriad of tasty ingredients: red lotus paste, crushed almonds, melon seeds, orange peel and sweetened cassia or lotus root. There is also a savoury alternative with ten-thousand-year eggs and preserved beef.

Carolyn's taste buds reject almost all varieties of moon cakes. She finds the lotus paste filling just about edible. Observing her stoically chewing her way through lotus paste, surreptitiously picking out lotus seeds, her eyes narrowing into scrunching slits, once again jolts my psychological understanding of trans-cultural chasms virtually impossible to bridge. I suddenly realise I am unable to provide a recipe for baking moon cakes. Many apologies for raising false hope.

This chapter ends on a very pleasant childhood reminiscence of tropical weather. I started this chapter writing about weather. Weather temperate and tropical feels like a Gestalt whole. Perhaps I, too, have begun to be obsessive about weather.

On several heavy, dew-laden tropical dawns, I would accompany my father and his business partners on an inspection of their rubber estate in Malaysia. If a tropical storm was brewing, there would be a need for flaming torches to light up the long dark avenues of stalwart rubber trees. On sunny days, the heavy mists would quickly dissolve and daylight would seep through. So unlike the misty autumnal mornings in Norfolk, where low-hanging clouds and mist would provide a shroud of greyness, often lasting throughout the day. Consistent English grey days of damp and depression are exacerbated by dripping, carry-on-regardless rain; again, so unlike the short tropical bursts of rain.

We would start the inspection when there was sufficient light. The estate manager would take us methodically down and up each avenue of trees that had been tapped that morning. Each tree would have a fresh incision and a gentle stream of milky white, rubbery fluid would be flowing or dripping into the clay collecting pots. The hypnotic stillness of walking between repeated regimented rows of bleeding trees would occasionally be broken by sharp protestations from tappers accused of diluting latex or fixing the hydrometer.

I have a grandiose reminiscence that, even as a child, I had found my specialty calling of psychiatry, as I would then interfere in the argument to defuse the distress of the accused male or female tapper by acting the fool pleading for leniency. My father would then sharply clip me behind my ear. The estate manager, however, would be indulgent of adolescent interference and pretend to listen to my case. He was a man from East Anglia, though I now wryly remember I did not then know where East Anglia was!

It would be mid-morning when all weighing and collection procedures were completed. We then proceeded to the factory where rubber sheets were rolled out. A heavy odour suffocated the atmosphere. Then the moment I relished on every trip: The inspection task completed, my father, his business partners and the estate manager would retreat into the shade to have a *stengah* or two of scotch.

A few tappers were corralled to take me for a swim in a murky pool filled with stagnant rainwater from the last monsoon. My knowledge of tropical medicine has never been honed as well as my grasp of psychiatry, which was to my advantage as I never thought of the dangers lurking in the murky pool. Dengue, malaria, leeches, flukes.

During the fourth year of my medical studies, I had decided on my choice of specialty which was much earlier than most medical students who tend to reach a decision after completing their Pre-Registration House Officer's postings. My wise mother said, 'Darling boy, as you are half mad already, go the whole way.' Thank you, Mumma, for encouraging me into a career I have enjoyed very much indeed. Unfortunately, friends disagree with my mother's opinion: they think I have always been totally mad to be as I am now.

Anyway, the tappers and I would strip off, jump into this fulminating quagmire and I would spend the next hour being hailed as a champion jouster. Totally fixed, as I was never let to fall off the taut, muscular shoulders of my steed, and all challengers made sure they did not push my fat and wobbly, fair adolescent body too hard when they shoved with their lithe, tanned, manly physiques.

Back in Norfolk, there is a pond set some distance from the village where I live. It is reminiscent of the murky Malaysian swimming hole. Thankfully, however, the mosquito-borne illnesses and parasites are not endemic in Norfolk. I have waded in this pond, kicked the algae, felt desperately alone and beat a quick retreat home to the reassuring sound of ice clinking in a glass of scotch, the warmth of a *stengah* being preferable to ankle-deep, icy water. I have become in many ways like my father in his love of all things country. There is in me to this day a lingering fondness for the smell of rubber sheets, a smell most people abhor.

Writing this section has brought me on a journey around my father and mother and rounded up jagged guilty feelings within me of having lived a long time away from my birthplace and the two of them. For this psychological closure, I am most grateful.

Winter

'Now is the winter of our discontent. Made glorious summer by this sun of York.'
William Shakespeare, Richard III

'One of my current pet theories is that the winter is a kind of evangelist. More subtle than Billy Graham, of course, but of the same stuff.'
Shirley Ann Grau (1929)

Winter unfortunately brings out the worst of my personality with an infelicitous exhibition of some stereotypical Chinese traits. I become gluttonous, melancholic, lascivious, often worse for drink and terribly superstitious. Fortunately, rural Norfolk does not provide gambling and opium dens for me to indulge in other well-established Chinese vices. I am limited to five deadly sins, a safe number. (I have already mentioned the import of the number five in my Fifth Season chapter.) But my Yin and Yang are at odds with each other. My personal *chi* and my bisected teardrop-shaped circle of dark and light, representing the Taoist doctrine of 'First the shadow, then the light', becomes unmercifully lowered and blurred. It is all shadows, very little light, reflecting winter's dim light.

Nature itself certainly does not help here. The countryside is gripped in a glove of darkness, interrupted only by episodes of fog, snow and black ice. A woman in our village has the reputation of being uncannily able to predict the severity of a winter, using cobwebs and spiders for divining. She is supposedly not a witch, and though she had received minimal education, she developed a surprising love for the works of William Blake.

In summer, she would count cobwebs with a filigree pattern akin to snowflakes. In early winter, she would only count cobwebs touched with a tinge of frost. Using an equation known only to her, she would obtain a definitive number involving winter and summer cobwebs. Did she add, subtract, divide or multiply? I have no idea. But based on this result, she could predict how the rest of winter would turn out.

There might be something in her method. As a Chinese symbol, spiders are creatures signifying good omens. When they slide down their webs on their homespun silken threads, they symbolise 'joy descending from heaven'. I am tempted to suggest this village lady's love for the works of William Blake explains her ability to identify with his declaration of being able to receive messages from heaven.

My first British winter kicked off in a very wet manner. It rained incessantly for three days and three nights. Every flat-lying field was waterlogged. I had bought a house built at the base of gently rolling fields in a hollow or depression, glibly thinking it was appropriate for a psychiatrist to live in a depression. Payback time. This foolish gesture now became a problem. Water from the surrounding fields crept steadily forward to surround the house.

On the fourth morning, I optimistically started calling myself Noah; I would survive a flood. But the time it took me to shave saw an alarming increase in water level. The local fire service was not at all helpful. They could not pump the muddy vortex away as all the surrounding fields were also under water. It was suggested that the local farmer should cross-plough his fields in future! This would apparently divert the water away from the lower parts of the land. I went to work leaving my part-time gardener as a rearguard. By midday, he summoned me home. I arrived to swirling eddies of gruesome brown water gurgling through the entire house.

I will always be indebted to the gardener as single-handedly, in true Herculean mode, he saved my scholar's bench, the carpet from my parents' house, all beds, chests of drawers and chairs. Books, shoes and records floated around, their paths blocked by bits of hitherto well-fitted carpets now floating about in the bubbling and steadily rising water. The village lane took on the appearance of the Chinese character for water, a central cascade with sprays or rivulets dashing out on both sides. A perfect pictogram.

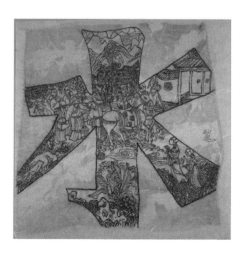

WATER POURED OUT
(SEE PLATE V)

45

There is a well-known Chinese story which has been adapted into a lesser-known opera: *Water Poured Out.* In this story, Scholar Zhu was a very poor man as he spent all his time at his desk, studying for examinations. His wife deserted him to marry the affluent butcher in the village. Zhu finally passed the state examinations and became a highly paid, high-ranking official. A tour of duty took him back to his home village. His social-scrubbing, upwardly mobile ex-wife, seeing a chance to further improve her status, ran out to meet him and begged to be taken back. Zhu remained seated on his horse and asked his servant for a container of water. He then poured the water out onto the ground which enchantingly took the form of the Chinese character for water. Zhu then declared 'Water poured out cannot return to the original container.' His ex-wife, in shame, committed suicide. Freud's theory of a 'death instinct' reflects the thinking of his time and is not particularly relevant to the presenting mental state of this particular scheming harlot. The commonly held theory that suicide is a reaction to the threat to one's acceptable life conditions and sense of competence, is perhaps more diagnostic within this fable. A loss of hope and FACE!

Water pouring in has a similar suicidal effect. Those of you readers who have suffered a flood or fire (the latter definitely worse) will empathise with me at the degree of immediate reactive depression and subsequent post-traumatic stress such an event creates.

The defensive quick response was simply to joke about the disaster. In other words, keeping the stiff upper lip. The Ancient Mariner provided words to maintain an outwardly jocular mental state as none were forthcoming in the numbed, withdrawn state I had retreated into. 'Water, water, everywhere, and all the boards did shrink. Water, water, everywhere, nor any drop to drink.' Not really amusing though.

Neighbours from the hill bundled me up beside their Aga stove. Unlike the all-encompassing Biblical flood, houses built on the upper side of the village were not affected by this deluge. The residents thereof fed me and filled me with scotch. My alcohol level rose steadily, but I could not get drunk. I left my shoes to dry overnight on their stove and so be ready for the weekly outpatient clinic. The shoes were to be my only dry pair for the morning's work. I refused their offer to stay and that of Carolyn's to bring my PJs over to her house. I could not stay away and leave my home suffering with such distress.

Stumbling into the pantry, I saw a box of soap powder which would sustain the washes of a month's laundry. I had to save it. The bottom fell out and a mountain of white powder bubbled merrily as if in an attempt to clean the muddy water. I sat down and howled.

The aftereffects when clearing up after the flood are, at best, awful as you are plagued by constant, unshakable thoughts of illness and disease. The muddy brown colour of the flood water was probably due to the main component: mud or—perish the thought—it could have reflected seepage from the sewage in the septic tanks. Over the next few weeks, my body was covered in sores and blemishes of unknown aetiology and I lost a stone in weight. It was indeed biblical in theatrical effect.

In retrospect, I realise that certain variables sustained me through the event:

- the kindness of neighbours and of being cared for by members of the village. They suggested I should throw my PJs in a bag and sleep over. My working shoes were dried on their Aga. The pleasurable anonymity of city life would not have provided this. This was the kindness from strangers acting predictably as good country

Samaritans and not as uninvolved city shadows;
- rote learning of poems at school;
- and a lesson remembered from Sunday School, not a Chinese fable! In this, we find Christ meeting the woman from Samaria by the well and her recognition of water interacting with Jesus as his being a symbolic representation of the well of eternal life and salvation.

It is well documented that in times of great stress, we fall back on our strongest beliefs for sustenance, and I am indeed lucky to have been well-grounded by my parents, my school and in my faith.

Time for a fable pulling together some of the many variables mentioned previously: arrows, beautiful maidens, torrents of water and a many-splendoured thing called love; in this instance, love at first sight.

Zhen Yi led his soldiers to the Yellow River for a short respite. He was impressed that the river had risen and formed an immense torrent. He playfully shot an arrow into the water. The waters parted and out sprang a man clothed in white, riding a horse and accompanied by a dozen attendants. Zhen Yi's company of soldiers cried out in fear at this apparition. He quickly shot a second arrow aimed at the man's left eye. The horseman immediately took flight, leaving behind a beautiful young maiden who happened to be the younger sister of the Spirit of the Waters. Zhen Yi shot a third arrow into her hair. She thanked him for sparing her life. Their eyes locked in a serendipitous alchemy of feelings and she agreed to be his wife. The wedding duly took place after Zhen Yi gained permission from the Emperor and the happy couple were married under an archway of arrows.

PLATE II
THE BALCONY SCENE
Wang Jianan and Cai Xiaoli

PLATE *III*
THE HARRIDAN
Wang Jianan and Cai Xiaoli

Plate V
Water Poured Out
Wang Jianan and Cai Xiaoli

PLATE VI
THE GHOST CATCHER
Wang Jianan and Cai Xiaoli

Plate VII
Iris Surrounded by Four Gentlemen
Wang Jianan and Cai Xiaoli

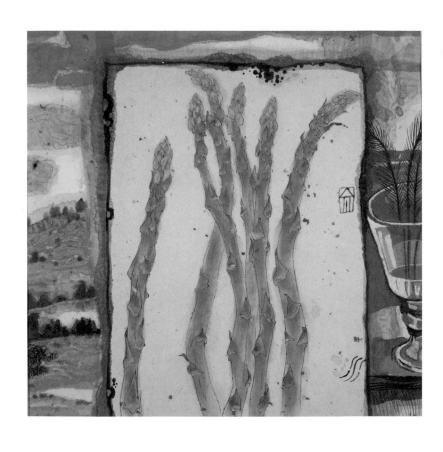

PLATE *VIII*
ASPARAGUS
Wang Jianan and Cai Xiaoli

PLATE *IX*
CELEBRATION OF TEA
Wang Jianan and Cai Xiaoli

PLATE X
EIGHT FAIRIES
Wang Jia Jia

PLATE XI
DRAGON'S GATE
Wang Jianan and Cai Xiaoli

PLATE XII
SCHOLAR CONTEMPLATING MONUMENTALITY OF MOUNTAIN RANGE
Wang Jianan and Cai Xiaoli

In this story there are many psychoanalytical images. Readers may work out their own interpretations. Tagging on personal meanings to symbols can be great fun and good for one's creative mind and cognition, similar to doing crosswords or sudoku.

Snow, a refined and sophisticated version of water, should be seen and experienced by everyone. It is magical and so beautiful. A black bag of garbage dumped unceremoniously on a concrete pavement, when covered with a dusting of snow, becomes transformed into a lovely sculpture. But snow can also be dangerous. Sometimes when Norfolk skies capriciously change from grey scuttling clouds to bright pink and lavender clouds heavy with snow, the undulating plains can soon be covered by deep snow which quickly drifts and becomes a major hazard. For this reason, snow dunes are frighteningly beautiful.

Above all, snow is transient and ultimately melts. Chinese painters have traditionally captured snow in paintings, especially paintings of mountains and rivers, as a record of its magic. My artists flatly refused the request to add to the bountiful trove of snow paintings. Instead, they encouraged me to develop the next paragraph on ghosts as they were at that point determined to paint ghosts.

Indeed, they knew they were playfully feeding into my already unstable melancholic winter psyche caused by the never-ending long, dark days and swirling mists. Ghosts are the nemesis of all Chinese. We have categories of demons, spirits, hungry spirits, fairies and ghost traffic. The logical mind becomes unhinged if a ghostly presence is felt.

I myself had the misfortune of previously owning a fifteenth-century weekend cottage with a resident ghost. The quick purchase of said weekend home was based on the quaint English imagery of ancient beams, thatched roof and inglenook fireplace.

On completion of the contract of sale, the previous owner, a jolly games mistress who kept her hockey stick under her bed to thump would-be burglars, presented me with a gift of a book that she thought would be of interest to me. It was a completely innocent and generous gesture on her part which turned into a major trans-cultural difficulty for me. This Wiltshire book of ghosts documented a phantom, The Grey Lady, as a permanent resident in my newly acquired cottage.

Jolly-Hockey-Sticks admitted to having seen her once and thought it was great fun. Having a resident ghost had also pushed up the asking price by a couple of thousand pounds. What, what, what?

The Grey Lady is reported to have lived in the cottage sometime in the sixteenth century and was the wife of the local carter. Whenever he was out delivering farm produce, she would apparently seduce village boys. On an early return, he discovered his wife in bed with a hapless lad and slit her throat. Her hungry spirit still roams the cottage. Friends with psychic sensitivity or neuroses experienced her presence. On a weekend visit, Carolyn's cousin Nigel, my solicitor, reported feeling oppressed as he felt someone sitting on his body during the night. A friend visiting from Hawaii suggested hanging a sign with the catchphrase 'Jesus Lives' in the upstairs corridor, the place where she strongly felt the presence of the Grey Lady.

Thankfully, I never had a sighting of the lady and have to admit shamefacedly that I have never stayed overnight in the cottage on my own. After this experience, I was sensible enough when shipping out of Wiltshire to buy a Norfolk home chosen on the basis of being a ticky-tacky cattle shed conversion where the only ghosts haunting me would be dead cows.

The artists then turned around and decided they were not about to paint ghosts, but said they would like to paint the seminal ghost catcher of Chinese folklore, Zhong Kui, to add to the smaller catalogue of paintings on this subject. I agreed to support this academic aim as they have steadfastly supported all my demands and whims. However, I soon learnt that Zhong Kui had committed suicide after the Emperor stripped him of his top examination honours due to his disfigured appearance. Whilst in purgatory and fuelled by his resentment against the Emperor, he steadily worked his way to becoming King of Ghosts in Hell.

During the Tang dynasty, he achieved his folkloric popularity, as one of the Tang emperors became gravely ill and had a dream. The content of the dream involved two ghosts. The smaller of the two ghosts stole a purse from the Imperial Consort and a flute belonging to the Emperor. (Once again, there has to be some psychoanalytical interpretation here!) The bigger ghost, with the help of his sword, captured the smaller ghost, tore out his eye and ate it. *Aiyoh!* A beastly image for me, when I was a child. This illustrates some of the imagery discussed by psychoanalysts in the origins of nightmares.

The bigger ghost then introduced himself in the dream as Zhong Kui and pledged to heal the Emperor's illness. When the Emperor awoke, he had recovered from his illness and Zhong Kui was raised to the status of a Door God in the Tang dynasty, stationed at the back door of houses to keep illness from re-entering the home. Full reparation was therefore achieved by Zhong Kui as he was now a benign ghost-catcher. Within some circles of Western designers, his new benevolent status is incorporated as a decorative item for good *feng shui*. This is an example of intercultural confusion, rationality gone to the dogs. The painting is my least favourite, and sometimes I think the artists are not really nice people as they have not included the 'good luck' bat which tempers most paintings of this renowned ghostbuster.

THE GHOST CATCHER
(SEE PLATE VI)

Winter has the advantage over the other three seasons of hosting two major celebrations, Christmas and Chinese New Year. The latter is determined by the lunar cycle and is a moveable feast occurring sometime between mid-January and mid-February. Chinese New Year celebrations last for fifteen days and overshadow the single non-lunar New Year's Eve. My mother was always in a hypomanic state by the twenty-third of December. Perhaps it was a recurrence of the state she had been in when I was in her womb and she had hoped for a son (after two daughters) and a Christmas child?

Her energies were now channelled into decorating home and hearth. Was this her need to compensate for not having a Christmas Day child? Frankly, I am glad I missed arriving on the 25th, as I have enough psychological baggage and do not need the additional onus of having been born on Christmas Day.

The miniature Christmas fir tree was brought in by the gardener. Not too early, so as to be just right for Christmas Day as the tree would lose its sheen in the house. My mother's two maids would help dress the tree according to the year's grand design. Somehow, crepe papers of green and red were incorporated yearly. Christmas colours learnt from the English matrons when my mother was a trainee nurse? Turkey, ham and all the trimmings were served on Christmas Eve, accompanied by my father's annual comment that cranberry jelly spoils the taste of the meats; chilli sauce should be served instead. My mother turned a dutifully deaf ear.

This traditional ritual of arousal took place in sweltering temperatures in the high eighties. My childhood knowledge of snow was that of cotton wool balls and glitter spray. A clear correlation, no doubt, to the strong view I have expressed of experiencing real snow.

Another magical experience with an equal 'wow' factor which may be very personal to me: Wherever I am on Christmas Eve, shivering or sweating, cold sober or worse for drink, at the stroke of midnight, entering into the threshold of Christmas morning, I know I hear the singing of the angelic hosts.

By Chinese New Year's eve, my mother was again in a full-blown manic state and this presenting mental state had no correlation to me or my impending birth. Mother! All Chinese households are caught in a whirling dervish-like swirl of activity, gathering together every single item symbolising good luck. Red is the colour of the festival. There are red sashes, banners, clothes, shoes and bright red envelopes, much appreciated by every child as the contents can seriously inflate pocket money.

Food has to have names denoting good luck. Thus we have a black hair-like algae, *fa cai*; fish, or in Chinese, *yú*, a word sounding like 'surplus of'; and abalone, a much-treasured New

Year's delicacy, as a dish of bird's nest soup is favoured for other celebrations. And it's not just the names of foods that suggest good luck: rhyming couplets are stuck on doorways with the mandatory red fabric.

I still honour these superstitious rituals in Norfolk every Lunar New Year's eve. However, that year of the flood, I must have forgotten a good luck ritual which could have prevented the tragedy. Which ritual did I not carry out? *Mea culpa, mea culpa, mea maxima culpa.*

There is the ritual of turning on every light within the house just before midnight to herald in the Lunar New Year with light. I must have missed switching on a light bulb somewhere along the way. Perhaps extremely critical for good fortune in the dense darkness of the prolonged winter night.

Spring

'In spring at the end of the day, you should smell like dirt.'
Margaret Atwood (1939–)

At last, the clocks jump forward by an hour to British summer time, meaning more daylight hours and less misery for many, meaning happier people supposedly. Yet it is well established that there is a spring peak of clinical depression. Strange, no? Somehow the renewal of life and light in nature's spring, where a grey, drab world bursts forth with promise, paradoxically causes feelings of alienation and disruption amongst some individuals, resulting in a clinical depressive episode. The human psyche never fails to amaze. Which is why I have been held spellbound by my chosen profession.

Common lyrical (i.e. non-clinical) terms to describe this syndrome include: down in the mouth; feeling blue; being low in spirits; suffering from a great deal of unhappiness; sinking into sadness; exhibiting symptoms of a clinical depression; and, ultimately, unremitting despair when life starts to lose its meaning.

Interestingly, the Chinese language and dialects offer only limited terminology for depression. My personal favourite is 'choked heart'; well-chosen words to balance the moods.

Obviously, the Chinese believe that before you confront a beast, you must make it beautiful. This lack of descriptive phrases for depression in Chinese culture may also indicate an avoidance of a subject that is so, so sorrowful and as difficult to make beautiful as a purse out of a sow's ear.

There is obviously some major disconnect between the outside environment and the inner being here. In spring, the English countryside is at its best as, predictably, snowdrops, daffodils and bluebells make their reappearance, as they have from time immemorial. It is, or should be, a time for renewing one's love of the English countryside. The very essence of spring is captured by the fragile snowdrop, the daffodil with its robust, determined yellow nodding heads and the elegant bluebell. This floral trio parallels the three so-called gentlemen plants in Chinese culture which represent the essence of life: bamboo, orchids and plum blossom.

Each of these Asian plants represents an important human trait. For instance, bamboo, even in snow, grows straight upwards and is thought to characterise a just, loyal and trustworthy person. The orchid, meanwhile, has a subtle aroma and represents a person of elegance, refinement and gentleness. In times of uncertainty, when a change of dynasties was taking place, scholars would paint orchid plants without roots, denoting a time of change. Although gentlemen were not supposed to openly express disruptive feelings, those orchids without roots offered a covert message of dissention. A quiet rebellion.

The plum blossom with its voluptuous five petals symbolises a sensual and sexual person with a need to propagate. In ancient days, when Emperors reigned, the Five Clans (consisting of Chinese, Manchus, Mongolians, Mohammedans and Tibetans) would use bed covers embroidered with plum blossoms and fruit to imply sexual pleasure and encourage procreation. In modern

Republican times, the Five Clans are disparate and a one-child philosophy has become law for the majority members of the clan; so much for procreativity.

The average English person is always disposed to siding with the perceived underdog and current politics involving the Five Clans has become a major subject of debate. This was especially evident with the 2008 Beijing Olympics. Having grown up under a very safe political regime and thus not being political astute, I hold on without expressing any political opinion and continue the practice of painting these three gentlemen flowers. After all, a gentleman never openly creates a dissonant milieu. Not a good Chinese gentleman, in any event.

According to the definitive guide for Chinese brush painting, *The Mustard Seed Garden Manual of Painting*, the basic brush strokes of Chinese painting are learnt by painting these same three flowers, with the addition of a fourth flower, favoured, too, by the literati: the chrysanthemum. This manual states that painting the chrysanthemum flower adds to the scholar's ability with ink and brush as it necessitates holding in one's heart the Taoist concepts of truth, nature and inner power. All of the four flowers translate into brush strokes which capture the contrary challenges of structural formality and free-flowing spirit, which is the soul of Chinese painting.

Some of my Chinese kinsmen insist that a set of four panels of paintings depicting bamboo, plum blossom, orchid and chrysanthemum (readily available in art shops) represent only the four seasons without denser turgid symbolism and they caution me that I am once again reading and interpreting too much symbolic meaning there. However, my artist friends refused to take up the cross-cultural challenge of painting yellow daffodils, blue bluebells and white snowdrops in Chinese black ink brushstrokes for this book; to them, such a painting would only take on a cartoonish value. Instead, they have produced for me an exquisite painting of an iris held by a border of the four gentlemen friends.

IRIS SURROUNDED BY FOUR GENTLEMEN
(SEE PLATE VII)

Back to spring. This is, of course, the season of intensive gardening activity: planting, hoeing, pruning, hedging, cutting. A love of gardens is shared by both English and Chinese cultures. A benevolent spirit of gardening exists strongly in both cultures. The English believe that gardeners deprived of their artistry in the garden will be judged only by the resonance of their solitude or the quality of their despair. The Chinese would certainly understand this. There is a Chinese saying: 'To be happy for a week, roast a pig; but to be happy forever, plant a garden.'

Tao Chien of the Six Dynasties is credited with the philosophy of the garden as a timeless paradise. In one fable, *Peach Blossom Spring*, he writes about a fisherman on a fine spring day, whilst totally focused on trying to land a catch, drifted downstream a long, far distance. Suddenly, he saw a dense grove of blossoming peach trees planted along the bank stretching for miles. No tree of any other kind broke this span. The peach blossom, fragrant, delicate and almost translucent to his eye, fixed his visual field. In the gentle spring gust of wind, the air was filled with fluttering, drifting peach blossom. The world around him ceased to exist. Preoccupied with the minutiae of these flowers, he heard birds sing and mindlessly began to chant 'Flap, flap, the wind blows my gown. I have achieved true contentment in this place.' He had crossed into a different time sphere.

I am very lucky indeed to have viewed the New York Metropolitan Museum of Art show 'Peach Blossom Springs', an exhibition of gardens and flowers in Chinese paintings. I strongly recommend the catalogue of this exhibition, if available, as it clearly describes the essence and meaning of gardens for all Chinese people. In leafing through this book, you can even acquire some sympathy for the fisherman.

Despite being from two different cultures, as fellow garden-lovers, Carolyn and I move as one into a land where worldly time has stopped. Frequently in spring, I have to force Carolyn away from her herbaceous borders, weeds and vegetable patch, struggle to get her into the house for an evening meal and then nag her to remain for a while in our time. Despite all my efforts, she sits there smiling with a satisfied, almost psychotic cheerfulness, suspended in a personal space of her garden. Following Margaret Atwood's counsel, she smells of dirt.

Spring also sees my menagerie of animals increase, as it were, by several foals and fold. Bleating lambs, tadpoles, ducklings, baby pheasants, cygnets, bats and fawns all appear. On a nearby estate, a tableau of young fawns nestling against adult doe and deer, set against the sharp new green of spring, is similar to the frequently reproduced porcelain vases glazed with one hundred deer.

The deer is evidently an excellent symbol for spring and all it promises. The reason? Deer apparently live to a very great age and deer also happen to be one of the Chinese symbols of longevity. It is also said to be the only animal capable of rooting out the sacred fungus of immortality.

Deer horn is mentioned in Chinese and European pharmacopoeia as a means of prolonging life. The older population living on the north Norfolk coast must have a steady supply of this elixir stashed away somewhere. Large swathes of the coastline have been christened Costa Geriatrica.

Another feature of spring in my adopted homestead is the appearance of bats. Somehow, with the growing light, they become a more visible population. On most evenings by the local church, bats swirl and swoop against the fading spring evening sky. Coincidentally, these heavenly rats feature prominently in Chinese folklore. One reason is that the word 'bat' in Chinese sounds like the word for 'good fortune'. Bats represent five blessings: longevity, riches, health, praise of virtue and a good death.

I owe a great deal of my understanding of the symbolic meanings of Chinese life to Professor Wolfram Eberhard's *Dictionary of Chinese Symbols*. I have read and reread this important reference dictionary, always with great pleasure and unflagging interest. I have learnt a great deal from it. At times, I may even subconsciously quote his hue of definitions in my book and hope that the late professor, his estate and publishers will accept that 'imitation is the best form of flattery.'

Oh yes, a *good* death. As a race, we Chinese are afraid of becoming hungry ghosts, i.e. ghosts of people with unrequited, unfulfilled, searching for contentment, lives. Ghosts who would not find salvation.

There is a strong opinion that death given as a sacrifice, even for a noble cause, still results in becoming a wandering hungry ghost. The following story illustrates this.

Once upon a time in Beijing, a young girl sacrificed her life for her father. He was the most skilful bell-maker in China. Unfortunately, a commission from the Emperor turned out dreadfully wrong. Each time the clay mould was broken, there was a flawed bell, without a clear ringing sound. The bell-maker would lose his life if the third bell was not perfect. Just before the large cauldron of molten metal was emptied into the mould, the filial daughter jumped into the bubbling larva. Everyone cried and shrieked as they knew she was trying to fulfil the formula of perfect metal requiring a maiden's blood. There was nothing to be seen of the girl except for her shoe clutched in her nanny's hand. This faithful retainer had rushed forward to catch the girl as she jumped. To this day, it is still believed that after each clear peal of bells in Beijing, there comes the whisper 'Shhhoe-h', which is the hungry ghost calling for her lost shoe.

I am personally terrified of all species of ghosts, hungry or otherwise, and therefore return once again to this topic. As a psychiatrist, madness is understandable to me as it is generated from within the mind; but spirits and possession! My fear must also be correlated to the swirling Norfolk mists.

So why do I retell this story? Well, despite all the prolific rebirth associated with the season, spring, for me, is also a time of death. Psychiatrists have patients they admire, and the springtime death of a particular county lady will always be remembered each time spring comes around.

This lady had stoically accepted the diagnosis of her failing cognitive functions. As her memory began to deteriorate further, she described herself as a distressed pilgrim on the road of life. Then, for no identifiable medical cause, her physical health began to fade. Largely undaunted, she continued to chomp on her pipe and drink her scotch, a very healthy *stengah*.

One spring night, she died peacefully in her sleep. She just gave up, gracefully. She had spent her life caring for others; in her time, she supported revolutions and wrote of her men who had a strong wish to ensure that freedom of speech, rights, honour and love continued in their particular spheres. Arming revolutionaries with guns, bakers with flour, authors with ink and always being the muse for her men, she loved each one for what they were about. None of them knew what or whom would finally mastermind their destinies. She wrote of these potent experiences and her writing will serve as her epitaph.

> *'Thou, too, art poor, like the spring rain*
> *that falls like a blessing on the roofs of the town;*
> *And like a wish nurtured by prisoners*
> *in a cell eternally deprived of the world,*
> *And like the sick who change their position in bed*
> *and are happy,*
> *Like the flowers along the railway line*
> *so grievously poor in the mad winds of journeys;*
> *and as poor as the hand into which we weep.'*

Each spring, I stand on the edge of a hill and genuflect to the broad white Norfolk skies in respect to her spirit. I also still mourn each spring for my mother. I bow, too, to honour all mothers and women who care for others in their special feminine manner, the scent of jasmine and womanhood.

This is a fitting reflection for this chapter as the Chinese Earth Mother *Ti Mu* is held responsible for the creation of the caring cycle and the birth of creativity all captured within spring.

A recurring theme throughout this chapter is that of renewal.

Nowhere is this theme more challenging then at Eastertide when the touchstone premise of Christianity, that of resurrection, is raised. Tied to the lunar calendar and the vernal equinox, Easter always occurs during spring.

On silent, misty Easter mornings, it is easy to capture the imagery of the women making their way to the sepulchre. The white, almost pure light of an early Norfolk dawn once again conjures up the crack of dawn spreading over rubber estates and, for me, weaves the threads of mothers, fathers and sons into a comforting, tightly bonded knot.

It also belies the Chinese belief that death given as a sacrifice results in becoming a wandering hungry ghost. For Christians, Easter signifies both the ultimate sacrifice and the ultimate triumph over death.

I am sounding a bit flat, sad, even a tad unhappy; an overall lowering of my affect. But I would like to end this chapter on a happier note. For all Singaporeans, an upbeat turnaround has to involve food. So let's turn to a favourite spring food.

Even a non-foodie like myself waits in eager anticipation for the flowering of asparagus at the end of spring. I mark this glorious short season by driving home most evenings past the asparagus farm to buy a kilo or more of tender, green-tinged asparagus with purple stalks. A bunch of the stalks take on the porcelain glaze called *san cai*, literally translated as three colours: green, aubergine and yellow or blue.

Besides being aesthetically pleasing, the taste is scrumptious. The asparagus is also touted as an aphrodisiac. We do not need Dr Freud to tell us that part of the belief has to do with its physical shape. Steamed, boiled, grilled, dipped in butter, in hollandaise sauce, wrapped with parma ham, in any number of ways, it is lip-smacking delicious.

A visit to the toilets of every gentlemen's club will tell you that spring has arrived as the smells of asparagus fill these areas at the height of the season. This is due to the pungent metabolic breakdown of this vegetable which comes out during urination. This probably holds for the private stronghold of ladies' clubs too. The former I can certainly vouch for; as for the latter, unfortunately, Carolyn refuses to comment.

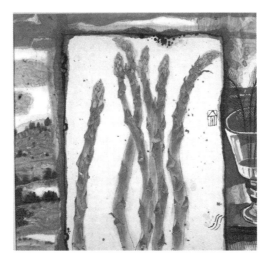

ASPARAGUS
(SEE PLATE VIII)

Summer

'Summer is the time when one sheds one's tensions with one's clothes and the right kind of day is jewelled balm for the battered spirit. A few of those days and you can become drunk with the belief that all's right with the world.'
Ada Louise Huxtable (1921–)

Sounds idyllic, doesn't it? Unfortunately, one is *not* happy despite it being summer and all is *not* right. Ms Huxtable writes with the easy confidence of a Pulitzer Prize winner. I write from a background of thought disorder and jostling imagery. Feedback from friends on the early drafts of this book was that its contents were one-dimensional. It was obviously easy to correlate English experiences with Chinese subconscious themes. But from me, these friends expected in-depth psychiatric descriptions of crucial levels of feeling and emotions when engaging with the English countryside. Finally, I am about to attempt this, as summer does conjure up a multiplicity of feel-good images.

'Summer in the countryside is a time of great emotional conflict. Weather is at best unpredictable, and there is serious longing amongst all souls for continuous warm days and steady sunlight. Summer often lets the collective psyche down, unlike the other seasons with the predestined certainty of steely grey coldness. Picnics and other outdoor activities planned during summer months inevitably beat a retreat indoors. Great disappointment and angst result.'

That was me, not some Pulitzer Prize winner. I am sure I should abandon these attempts at literary immortality and return to just exploring the comforting relationship of the two cultures. In other words, my many-splendoured thing, which acts as a balm to my battered spirit in the framework of the reassuring childhood warmth of stretches of hot summer days.

Carolyn copes with the heat by wandering around deliciously in sundresses and spends her time in the shade making nonsensical items for village fêtes and Women's Institute strawberry teas while I darken in the intermittent sun, both in mood and in flesh tones.

On very hot, still summer days, we quarrel. We have identified the triggering factors: wasps, bees, gnats, nettles and pollen, which suggests that the British live in a safer environment in terms of what fellow creatures they fear. The five poisonous creatures Chinese are afraid of are the lizard, centipede, scorpion, spider and toad. The first of these five is thought to be the most dangerous. It is capable of losing its tail, which can somehow wriggle its way into a person's auditory chamber and cause deafness. In many Chinese households, storage jars containing rice and salt have to be covered tightly as a lizard crawling over grain and condiments means instant poisoning. A simple lizard was therefore given monstrous properties; Freud would have had a great old time putting his phallic interpretation on all this. It is so good to write about the subconscious connection and symbolism whilst being one-dimensional. Balderdash!

Long, soporific weekend summer afternoons are frequently punctuated by the rhythmic click-click of cricket balls as the ball spins from bowler to batsman. Great expanses of green pitches are dotted with men in their whiter-than-whites. Raucous triumphant shouts erupt when a cricketer is bowled out or when a googly has been executed—a state of delightful pleasure which can also be induced by crickets.

Crickets are summer insects and in olden times, the Chinese literati would sit in the shade holding cricket containers close to themselves to hear the cricket's song. Gourds were often inserted inside a ceramic mould to be impressed by a pattern and form the container. From these decorated cages, the chirruping click-click would remind scholars that it was summer again and so time to pen another poem on crickets as emblems of courage. Penning these poems was a kind of competition to mark the refinement of being a gentleman. Cricket is, of course, a 'gentleman's game' and during both gentlemanly activities, a great deal of tea is drunk.

Ah yes, tea drinking. Perhaps I still have a chance to redeem myself as a writer of some depth and insight by exploring the cultural and psychological underpinnings of the British and Chinese approaches to tea and what these underpinnings signify. However, a person does not really need to be a psychiatrist to define the shared animus of both cultures for tea.

Both the British and Chinese cultures have strong traditions of consuming a great deal of tea. In the United Kingdom, however, tea is largely drunk without much discernment or ceremony. A 'cuppa' drunk from breakfast onwards is usually tea made from a tea bag, sloshed with milk and sometimes heavily laden with sugar as if to mask the taste of the tea itself. A beverage signifying comfort and ritualistic habit. A slightly more refined way to drink tea in Britain (despite the ubiquitous tea bag) is to have it with a slice of lemon.

The Victorian tradition of tea served in fine bone china has all but disappeared. Teas back then were for showing off one's manners. But radical egalitarism, political correctness and dumbing-down pragmatism has put a stop to such genteelness.

When I first arrived in London as a very young trainee, I would sit in the homes of elderly patients with my community nursing team members and carry out a psychiatric assessment around tea. The anxiety of being a very clumsy man, balancing tea cups and saucers and trying very hard to avoid repeating the scenario of the Mad Hatter's tea party took the edge off my therapeutic skills.

As a consultant, I have resorted to banning tea-centred assessments. I tell colleagues that if drinking tea had a culture as with the Chinese ceremony, I would be prepared to reconsider.

There is an Asian, Chinese or Japanese tea culture that does not exist in Britain or even on the Continent. Preparation methods, the care taken with tasting, and the occasions which highlight the symbolic importance of appreciating tea make it almost an art form. There is the tea ceremony at traditional Chinese weddings, the practice of which fills up depleted coffers of the wedding couple as each cup of tea respectfully and filially served to relatives and respected family friends is rewarded by a good luck packet containing money. Tea also plays a significant role in ceremonies for birthdays, the Lunar New Year and other auspicious events.

White, green, black, oolong: elaborate romantic names further enhance matching tastes. Thus, we find teas with names like White Peony, Silver Tip, White Gunpowder, Green Dragon, Dragon Well Green, Lapsang Souchong, Black Keemum, Yellow Gold, Ti Kuan Yin. Magical, fairy-like names for an entrenched concrete ritual. Asian tea, though consumed by the wide populace, has a rooting in strong appreciation of the drink as ritual, not just as a strong 'cuppa'.

CELEBRATION OF TEA
(SEE PLATE IX)

Compact, magical summer nights are filled with fairies. Shakespeare gave us Peach Blossom, Cobweb, Moth and Mustard Seed, who produced jewels and sang enchanting songs. They were also, of course, great Bottom-feeders.

EIGHT FAIRIES
(SEE PLATE X)

Chinese folklore gives us the legendary eight fairies:

- He Xiangu
- Cao Guojiu
- Li Tieguai
- Lan Caihe
- Lu Dongbin
- Han Xiang Zi
- Zhang Guo Lao
- Zhongli Quan

They carry gourds, limp on crutches, sing unintelligible songs and are always choked with ideas of immortality. My favourite fairy from this octet is Li Tieguai, particularly in the legend of the expedition made by the eight fairy immortals to explore the Kingdom of the Sea. Li is always represented with a crutch and a gourd of magic medicines. In other words, a fairy doctor.

He is recognised as a benefactor of the sick. He was originally handsome with a muscular physique that would have made the finals of a bodybuilding contest. During an intensive meditation session, his soul left his body to gain further instruction on Taoist lore from Lao Tze, one of the great teachers of Taoism. In order to protect his body, he instructed his disciple Lang Ling to keep guard over the soulless body for seven days. Unfortunately, after six days, his disciple was called to the deathbed of his mother. In order to leave at once, he cremated his master's body.

Consequently, Li's soul wandered aimlessly on his return, unable to re-establish himself in his original body. Ashes unto, and perhaps undone by, ashes. Finding an unattended corpse, Li inserted his wandering spirit through the dehydrated beggar's nostril and made off, only to find himself in a body with an ulcerated leg, a cyclopic eye and an unruly woolly beard. The gods took pity and provided him with a crutch. My favourite fairy hence bears the monikers of 'Li with the Iron Crutch' and 'Li Hollow-Eye'.

His big adventure was as a result of the decision of the Big-Eight to explore the wondrous asymmetry of the sea, not to be found in their regular celestial sphere. Curiosity almost killed the cats in this episode. There was to be expected, much discussion over discarding the usual mode of celestial travel of sitting firmly on moving sacred clouds for a new method that would exhibit individual talents.

Each fairy pledged to place his or her precious emblem on the water and surf over the waves. Li threw down his crutch and gingerly stepped on it, having great difficulty keeping his balance, let alone trying to ride the wave. Zhongli followed suit on his fan, cutting a better style on the broad-based, feathered surface. Amidst great mirth, the other six followed suit. Unfortunately, on contact with the water, Cao's castanets turned into a singing melodic creature which attracted the attention of the Dragon King of the Eastern Sea. Accusing the eight of trespassing, he challenged them to a fight.

From our knowledge gleaned from kung fu movies, a single-skilled fighter (which the Dragon King must have been to throw such a quick challenge at our eight) can take on several opponents at a time; accordingly, an explosive fight ensued. Perhaps he picked up on their collective odd appearance and sensed an easy victory. Bully boy tactics! He was so right, as none of the fairies happened to be fighters and each suffered numerous injuries, which were then treated, comforted and almost instantaneously cured by Li's magic medicines.

When he felt that he had had a reasonable pugilistic work-out, Dragon King left the arena. Bowed but not bloodied and unscathed by pain, these eight fairies limped home to the heavens.

A simple psychological idea explains the dynamics of this tale: peer group support.

Tales of this journey, now known as 'The Outrage of Sea Life', spread through the heavens, detailing the great excitement of new experiences. An excitement I have myself experienced whilst living in Norfolk, with my muse and with my book.

I shake myself from the summer night's delusional fancy and pledge my love once more to this new excitement, the English countryside. Inspired by Shakespeare and Chinese legends, I rush across heavy dew-laden grass carried by a midsummer's dream and shout out to my other love, 'Carolyn, I love thee!' and immediately step on a nest of young nettles. Scathed with pain, I limp my way to bed. No longer cutting a romantic scholarly figure, but looking very much like the fairy doctor in need of an iron crutch.

Postamble

'Sisters don't need words. They have perfected a language of snarls and smiles and frowns and winks—expressions of shocked surprise and incredulity and disbelief. Sniffs and snorts and gasps and sighs—that can undermine any tale you're telling.'
Pam Brown (1948–)

As we have now reached the 'postamble', which signifies the end of this book, let me tell you a little more about myself. I have waxed lyrical about the influence of mothers and fathers in the previous chapters. However, with the exception of quoting Dr Freud, Rubenstein, Santayana and Shakespeare, I have used only contemporary, living female writers in the remaining quotes. There is a reason for this.

It is perhaps a Freudian subconscious need to acknowledge another major variable behind the drive to produce this book. I have five sisters; not four or six, but FIVE. I am third of the six of us siblings, having two elder sisters and three younger.

If I had been the only son at the head of the clan or even the youngest of six, I might have turned out different. There are numerous studies to show the effect of one's birth rank. Being the middle and sole male child and surrounded by women! Would I have otherwise been as disturbed and deviant? Would I have chosen psychiatry as my specialty? Surely the other specialities— surgery, radiology, ophthalmology, nephrology, neurology— conformed more to my parents' expectations for my medical training.

I love my sisters, but do not understand them. Individually, they are nothing to write home about, but as a whole, they form the complete woman; even more complete a female than Carolyn. As Pam Brown says, they can undermine any tale one is telling. Hence I have subconsciously repressed mentioning them till now. Yet they have in a way spurred me on to write this book as they do not think I have it in me to do so. I have not dedicated the book to you all, only to our parents, and I owe you one, girls!

What have I achieved with the publication of this book? Or, rather, what do I think I have achieved with this book?

- The immensely splendid paintings by my artist friends are now available for public appreciation;
- I have fallen back into the radar of re-acquainting myself with the best-loved Chinese folkloric tales;
- I have indulged in a longstanding fancy of creative writing and I have enjoyed tremendously, putting pen to paper in a non-scientific manner;
- It has been thought-provoking to work through Anglo-Chinese correlations and connections;
- I have fallen in love repeatedly with my muse and lingeringly with the imagery and offerings from my adopted countryside;
- I have had a great deal of fun writing this book and working with the editor. It has been as therapeutic as writing closure letters in cognitive analytical therapy.

I now realise I should have written a Chapter Eight for a very successful closure. I will be severely reprimanded by my publisher for dealing with the significance of the numbers four and five in the context of Chinese beliefs and missing out the significance of EIGHT, the seminal number eight for all and every Chinese. Eight in Chinese is *fatt* which is almost an onomatopoeic word as it resembles the action of a burst of good luck. It may affect book distribution and sales. I did contemplate not numbering 'Winter' as Chapter Four (with a convoluted explanation as to why I was doing so) and instead numbering it as Chapter Five. This 'postamble' would then have become Chapter 8. However, my acquired English rationale did not permit this adjustment. Hence I am leaving this book with seven chapters, not eight. *Fatt! Fatt! Fatt!* I am being silly and solipsistic!

But have I managed to capture the essence of the English countryside through Chinese eyes? Have there been any psychological insights of interest? Will further probes of contentment, creativity and an alleged everlasting harmony in the countryside of Yin and Yang—world without end, amen—define variables unavailable in the city? A feeling of safety when a person puts his or her trust in nature? I am not so sure. Readers may have become aware that 'Autumn' is the longest and strongest chapter of this book. This is in resonance to the disruptive emotions generated by the season. Circumstantiality's train of thoughts, over-inclusiveness, making of jam and chutneys, shutting down green houses and hyperactivity as a defence towards resisting hibernation as a person prepares for winter are defensive markers of this season.

I used as my literary model Dr Han in the hope her mixed heritage persona would give me strong inspiration when describing two cultures. Should I (being a true-blue Chinese) have used instead the lyrical poetess of the Song Dynasty, Li Zhi Zhou, who wrote with aching beauty? Would this book be a better read? I do not think so.

There is a seminal Chinese saying: 'It is possible even as a lowly carp to jump through Dragon's Gate and become a dragon when one has successfully overcome a hurdle.' This applied particularly to scholars who achieved success in post-graduate examinations. Has my writing passed the test, and this tome proven at least to be my many-splendoured thing? At least the last commissioned illustration, a collage of pure intense Chinese brush painting in the waves and paper cuts, certainly has achieved Dragon's Gate status.

DRAGON'S GATE
(SEE PLATE XI)

But all ventures must come to an end, a fitting end. So how should these ruminations end? I cannot better Shakespeare's lines to finish off with:

'I do love nothing in the world so well as you: is not that strange?

As strange as the thing I know not.'

(My English countryside)

And finally, as all psychiatrists have to have the last word (thanks to Freud and with apologies to the Bard), this is it: Every cohort of student writers; academics; authors; writers of postcards, diaries, letters to family, friends and occasional foes will all recognise THE greatest orgasmic moment ... that of putting in the last full stop.

SCHOLAR CONTEMPLATING MONUMENTALITY
OF MOUNTAIN RANGE
(SEE PLATE XII)

Select Bibliography

These are the books I frequently turned to, to evidence-base my material:

Barnhart, RM. *Peach Blossom Spring, Gardens and Flowers in Chinese Paintings* (The Metropolitan Museum of Art, 1984)

Burland, CA. *Ancient China* (Hulton Educational Publications, 1960)

Chiu, K (ed). *Chinese Fables* (The Peter Pauper Press, 1967)

Eberhard, W. *A Dictionary of Chinese Symbols* (Routledge & Kegan Paul, 1986)

Lai, TC. *The Eight Immortals* (Swindon Book Company, 1972)

———. *Treasures of a Chinese Studio* (Swindon Book Company, 1976)

Latsch, M-L. *Traditional Chinese Festivals* (New World Press, 1985)

Lin, Y. *The Chinese Theory of Art* (Panther Books, 1969)

Medley, M. *A Handbook of Chinese Art* (G. Bell & Sons Ltd, 1964)

Sze, M-M (ed). *The Mustard Seed Garden Manual of Painting* (Princeton University Press, 1956)

Tom, KS. *Echoes From Old China* (University of Hawaii Press, 1989)

Vaughan, JD. *The Manners and Customs of the Chinese* (Oxford University Press, 1971)

Ware, JR. *The Sayings of Confucius* (The New American Library Inc., 1955)

Werner, ETC. *Ancient Tales and Folklore of China* (Senate, 1995)

Williams, CAS. *Chinese Symbolism and Art Motifs* (Charles E. Tuttle Company Inc., 1974)

Wong, J. *Chinese Fairy Tales* (Peter Pauper Press, 1946)

Wong, YK. *Unlocking the Chinese Heritage* (Pagesetters Services Pte Ltd, 1990)